SPRING
A·C·R·O·S·S
AMERICA

SEYMOUR SIMON

HYPERION BOOKS FOR CHILDREN
NEW YORK

With love
for Benjamin Simon,
my new grandson
(born in the spring)

PHOTO CREDITS
Front jacket, back jacket, pp. 1, 2-3, 5, 6, 11, 21, 30-32 © 1994 Seymour
Simon; p. 8 © 1992 John Gerlach/Dembinsky Photo Associates; p. 10 ©
1994 Dominique Braud/Dembinsky Photo Associates; p. 13 © 1994 Skip
Moody/Dembinsky Photo Associates; pp. 14-15 © 1994 Bill Lea/
Dembinsky Photo Associates; pp. 16-17 © Tom & Pat Leeson/Photo
Researchers, Inc.; p. 18 © 1994 David Wrobel/Biological Photo Service;
pp. 22-23 © Francois Gohier/Photo Researchers, Inc.; pp. 24-25 © 1992
Willard Clay/Dembinsky Photo Associates; p. 26 © Ted Levin; pp. 28-29
© J. H. Robinson/Photo Researchers, Inc.; p. 31 (inset) © Alan & Sandy
Carey.

For information address Hyperion Books for Children,
114 Fifth Avenue, New York, New York 10011-5690.

Printed in Hong Kong by South China Printing Company (1988) Ltd.

FIRST EDITION
1 3 5 7 9 10 8 6 4 2

This book is set in 16-point Leamington.
Library of Congress Cataloging-in-Publication Data
Simon, Seymour
Spring across America / Seymour Simon
p.   cm.
ISBN 0-7868-0069-0 (trade) — ISBN 0-7868-2056-X (lib. bdg.)
1. Natural history — United States — Juvenile literature.
2. Spring — United States — Juvenile literature.   [1. Natural
history.   2. Spring.]   1. Title.
QH104.S53   1996
508.73 — dc20   95-8184

Spring sweeps up the American continent like an incoming ocean tide. On the average, spring flows one hundred miles northward each week. In three months, spring moves from the southern tips of Florida, Texas, and California to the northern edges of Maine and Washington.

Spring begins on the calendar on or about March 21, the spring, or vernal, equinox. On the equinox, day and night are of equal length all over the world and the Northern Hemisphere begins to slant more and more toward the sun. But the first day of spring on the calendar often does not feel like the first spring day. Early spring in the northern states is often cold and snowy, and winter seems reluctant to leave. But as early as mid-February, swelling buds on trees and the appearance of crocuses announce the arrival of spring.

Spring in America means heavy rains and late snows. It means birds flying north, trees and grasses pushing out new green leaves, wildflowers bursting into bloom, and the sound of spring peepers. Spring is a season of beginnings, a signal of a renewal of life across America.

The first signs of spring are often the flowers and stalks of skunk cabbage that appear in marshes and wet woods as early as late February. The skunk cabbage is one of the few plants that can produce enough heat when it is growing to help melt some of the ice and snow. A skunk cabbage has a flowering stalk, called a spadix, that looks like a small pineapple. The spadix is strong and large enough to break through any snow and ice that may linger on the ground. As the flower grows, it is protected by a hood-shaped leaf called a spathe.

In the eastern states, the inner parts of the spathe are reddish. But along the Pacific coast, such as in Washington, the flowers and the spathe are bright yellow, and the plant is called yellow, or American, skunk cabbage. Skunk cabbages have a strong putrid odor like decaying meat, which gives the plant its name. Early spring insects are attracted to the plant by its odor and color. As they crawl over the flowers, the insects carry pollen from the flower of one skunk cabbage to another. This is called cross-pollination and will help the plant produce seeds.

Black bears eat the yellow skunk cabbage throughout the growing season. But all parts of the plant — leaves, roots, and flowers — contain a substance that burns a person's mouth if chewed raw. Native Americans boiled the young green leaves of skunk cabbages in several changes of water so that they could be eaten, and they roasted and dried the roots to make a kind of flour.

The first voices of spring are heard in late February and early March from Florida to New England and from Louisiana to Wisconsin. They come from a little frog called the spring peeper, or *Hyla crucifer*. A peeper is just an inch long, with a light brown body, dark stripes on its hind legs, and a big X on its back. The tiny frog often perches on a hood of skunk cabbage near a pond or a spring pool. Hylas can cling to smooth leaves because the pads on their fingers and toes act as suction cups.

A male hyla's throat swells up like a balloon as it begins to peep-peep, about once every second. The male is calling to female peepers to come to the pond. When a female arrives, the frogs mate. Soon the female begins to lay eggs, one at a time, on plants in shallow water. The eggs are tiny black-and-white balls in a coat of jelly. In a few days, the female peeper lays hundreds of eggs. Many other frogs, toads, and salamanders lay eggs in ponds in the spring. Leopard frogs lay thousands of eggs in huge clumps. Toads lay long, double-stranded strings of eggs. Spotted salamanders lay small bunches of eggs.

By midspring, the peeper eggs hatch into short-bodied tadpoles, with gills and a tail. During late spring and early summer, the tail is absorbed and the gills disappear. Lungs develop, and arms and legs appear as buds. By midsummer, the peepers undergo an incredible change. The tadpoles become frogs that can live on land. Frogs, toads, and salamanders are called amphibians, because they have lungs and breathe air as adults but have gills and live in water when first hatched.

In early March in the Northeast and the Midwest, soft pussy willows and the cheery notes of the robin proclaim the arrival of spring. The first pussy willows sometimes come out in February even when snow lies on the ground. As the spring draws nearer, the silver-furred catkins change to gold. The catkins are a close-packed mass of tiny flowers without petals but heavy with yellow pollen. The pollen provides bees with some of their earliest food after the winter.

The first robin arrives after a winter spent in the warmer South or protected in deep evergreens and wooded spots in the North. The older males are now in full color, with red breasts and bright yellow bills. Females and younger males are paler. Robins seem to be everywhere in the spring—on the wet ground, in lawns, in open

fields, and on tree branches. After an early morning concert, the robin begins to search the ground for worms. It stands still and tilts its head. Suddenly it runs a few steps, darts at the ground, and pulls up a worm. Robins eat plenty of worms and insects and also lots of fruits and berries.

Robins build a bowl-shaped nest of mud, leaves, and roots and line it with grass. The female lays from four to six eggs of robin's egg blue. Nestlings have the spotted breasts of the thrush family, to which robins belong. The parents keep busy feeding their young and defending their nests against prowling cats or snakes. The mothers remain on their nests with their young at night while the males assemble in roosts nearby.

In March and April, the Great Smoky Mountains of Tennessee and North Carolina are a riot of color. White dogwoods and shad-bushes, pink azaleas and mountain laurels, colorful blossoms on fruit trees, and acres of wildflowers are blooming. Spring advances swiftly in the valleys, climbing higher and higher up the mountain-sides with each passing day.

Heavy spring rainfalls and fertile soil have helped plant and animal life survive in greater variety in the Smokies than anywhere else in America. About 150 different kinds of trees have been found and about 2,000 other kinds of plants. There are also more than fifty kinds of mammals, including black bears, foxes, bobcats, raccoons, and deer, and a great variety of birds, reptiles, and amphibians.

The Great Smoky Mountains are the highest of the ranges in the Appalachian mountain chain that stretches down the East Coast from Maine to Florida. Many peaks in the Smokies rise to more than 6,000 feet (1,800 meters). The Cherokees, Native Americans who first lived in the region, called the mountains the Great Smokies be-cause of the blue haze that often veils the summits. Spring in the Great Smokies is a burst of flowers and a renewal of animal life coming out after the winter.

Black bear cubs are born in the cold months of winter in the Northeast, inside a dark den in the ground or a cave. Even though the mother bear is heavier than a big person, a bear cub is only about as big as a kitten and weighs about a pound, much smaller than a human baby. At first the cub is helpless and can do little more than nurse. Bear milk is very rich, and the cubs grow rapidly. In a few weeks, the cubs develop a downy fur coat and get their first sharp teeth.

When the snows begin to melt in March or April, the mother finally leaves the den with her cubs. Since the cold and snow last later in northern places, bears in the North stay in their dens longer than those farther south. The cubs have grown many times larger, but they are still very small, weighing only five to ten pounds, less than an adult house cat. They have thick coats, and their claws are well developed. At the first sign of danger, the mother bear chases her cubs up the nearest tree. These cubs are in a tree in a forest in the Northeast.

The cubs go everywhere with their mother in the spring. They grow rapidly and play games with each other. One cub nips another and then runs away while the second cub chases behind. Often the chases will end up in the trees. Cubs sometimes get their mothers to join in the games. They eat and eat and get bigger and bigger. They will stay with their mother through the summer.

Once described as being a mile wide and a foot deep, the Platte River flows across western Nebraska until it joins the Missouri River. Its banks are surrounded by marshes and wet prairies. In late March and early April, half a million sandhill cranes along with two million other waterbirds come to the Big Bend, a seventy-mile stretch of the Platte River in Nebraska. They have flown here from their wintering places near the Gulf of Mexico.

The sandhill crane is a large bird, more than three feet high with a wingspan of over six feet. With an ash gray body and a head cap of scarlet red, the sandhill crane is one of the most beautiful of North American birds. Most sandhills travel north in the spring to breeding grounds in Canada and return south in the fall. The huge number of sandhill cranes along the Big Bend in April waiting to migrate northward is one of the world's most spectacular wildlife sights.

Cranes and other waterbirds feed in shallow waters and wetlands, where they eat insects, worms, tadpoles, frogs, small fish, and plant matter. Development of the Platte River for hydroelectric power and irrigation has decreased the flow of water and the numbers of birds that the river can support. A wildlife sanctuary has been set up along the Platte, but much more land must be set aside if the birds that use these great spring resting grounds are to survive.

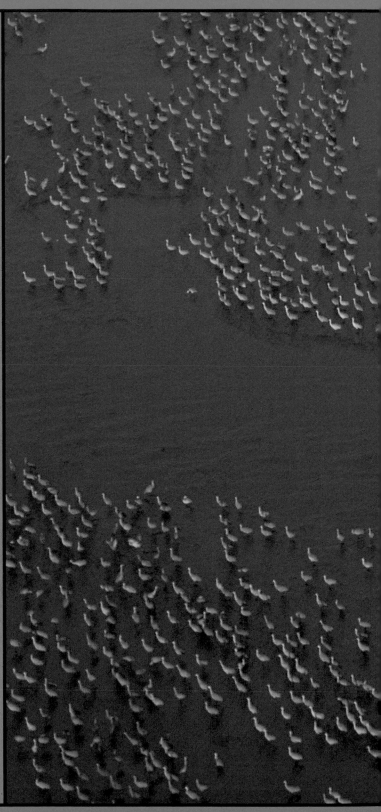

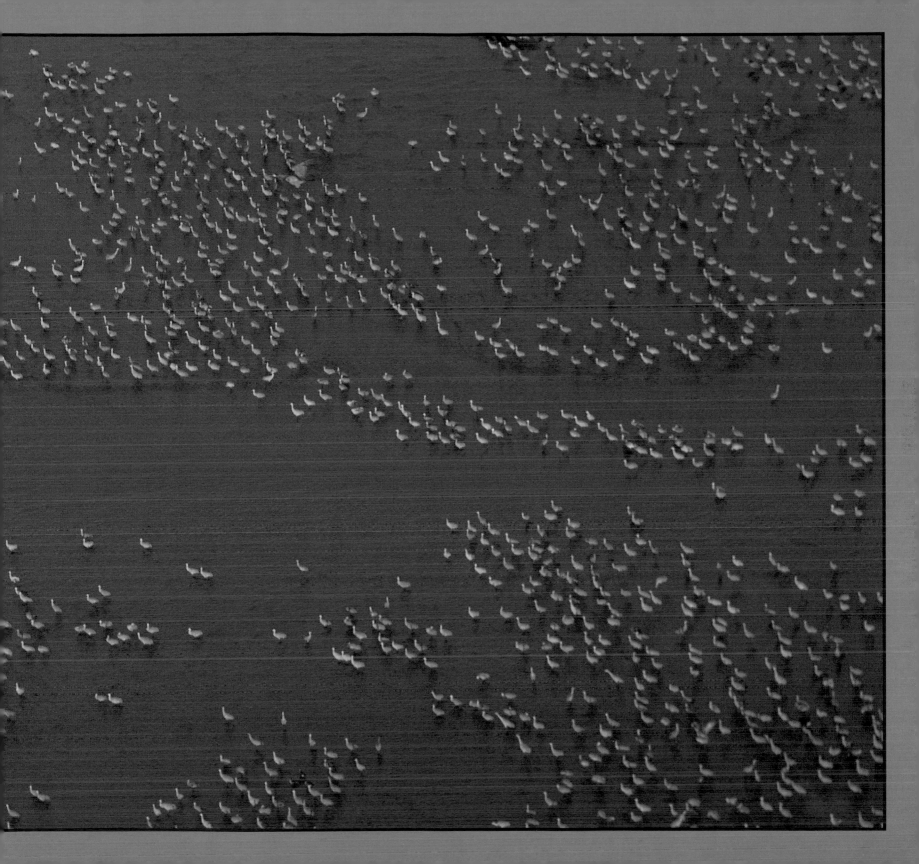

It is a late March night on the sandy beaches of Southern California and the spring tide is sweeping up the shores. The waters reach their highest point and then begin to ebb. A single slender fish, about as long as a pencil, rides in on the crest of the highest wave. Suddenly tens of thousands of fish sweep onto the beach. The wet sands are covered by wriggling masses of silvery fish.

It is the beginning of the yearly grunion run, when the fish come ashore with the spring tide to spawn. Spring tides have nothing to do with the season of the year. You can think of them as tides that "spring" up high. Spring tides are the highest high tides and the lowest low tides and come twice each month, at full moon and at new moon. From March until September, the grunion will come ashore at spring tides on certain Pacific beaches from Los Angeles south to Baja California. No one knows why the grunion choose some beaches rather than others. Some scientists think it is a combination of the water temperature and the type of sand.

As each female grunion is carried high up on the beach, she curves her body and pushes into the wet sand with her tail to lay her eggs. She squeaks as she wriggles in the sand. Perhaps it is this sound that attracts the male grunion that come in on the waves behind the females. Each male curves his body around a laying female and releases milt (fish sperm) that fertilizes the eggs. A few hours after the first fish come ashore, the grunion run ends. In two weeks, the young fishes hatch and are carried out to sea by the next high spring tide.

As the spring brings warmth and longer days, ferns begin to send up new deep, shiny green leaves in damp woodlands all across the country. Fern leaves are feathery and are called fronds. When fronds first appear aboveground, they are tightly curled together. As they begin to uncurl, the fronds look like the neck of a violin and are called fiddleheads. In some places in America, fiddleheads are boiled and eaten as greens. Fern leaves have a single midrib, with small leaflets branching off from either side. They grow from a creeping underground stem called a rootstock. These ferns are growing near a waterfall in the Cascade Mountains in Oregon.

Ferns, and their relatives the horsetails and club mosses, are non-flowering green plants. New ferns grow from tiny spores instead of from seeds. On the underside of a frond are clusters of brown dots. The dots, called sori, are made up of many spore cases, called sporangia. You can see a huge number of spores by placing a fern frond on a piece of white paper. After a day or two, lift the frond carefully. It will be outlined on the paper in a fine golden brown dust made up of millions of spores. Ferns go through two different kinds of reproduction. One generation grows from spores, and the next generation grows from a fertilized egg cell.

Ferns are part of an ancient group of plants that flourished before flowering plants appeared on the Earth. Even before the age of the dinosaurs, vast forests of giant ferns grew in swampy places. Over millions of years, the remains of the ferns turned into coal. Sometimes you can see the imprints of ancient fern leaves in the coal.

Red-sided garter snakes often hibernate during the winter in underground dens of dozens, hundreds, even thousands of snakes. If you
were to come upon a hibernating snake, you might easily think it
was dead. Its breathing is slow and shallow, and it has almost no
heartbeat. If you picked up a hibernating snake, it wouldn't react.
The snake uses up very little of the stored fat in its body for food
during hibernation. In this way, a hibernating snake is able to survive a long, cold winter when food is not easily available.

As spring days get longer all across America, garter snakes sense
the warmth and begin to awaken. Soon they move toward the light
and emerge from their dens. The males come out first. It is months
since the snakes have eaten. But before they eat, the males will stay
around the entrance to the den and wait for the females to come out.
The females come out in ones and twos. The females give off a
chemical, called a pheromone, that attracts the males. Each female
snake is soon surrounded by a mass of thirty to fifty males. Depend-
ing upon the location, the urge to mate lasts from early April until
late May, when the males go in search of food such as amphibians
and rodents.

Once mated, the female slips away. She spends the late spring
and early summer feeding and basking in the sun to hatch the eggs
inside her body. The young snakes, each fully formed and about as
thick and long as a pencil, are born about three months after mating.

Fields of bluebonnets spread across the hill country and prairies of Texas in May. Bluebonnets are small, deep blue flowers, clustered together at the end of a two-foot stalk. They have a central whitish or yellowish spot that turns red with age. Bluebonnets are native flowering plants of Texas. They flower year after year if left undisturbed. After heavy spring rains, bluebonnets and other flowers cover the hills in a riot of color.

Wildflowers grow all across America, in grasslands, atop mountains, along the edges of streams and glaciers, and in wetlands. The same kinds of wildflowers often grow together in groups because they have the same needs for light, soil, and water. For example, some kinds of wildflowers, such as trillium, bloodroot, and spring beauty, grow mostly in sheltered forests. Wildflowers that live in the shade store up food within their bulbs and rootstocks, so they have less need of sunlight to make food. They grow close to the ground and flower early in spring before new tree leaves cut down their light.

Some American wildflowers are becoming rare. When land is cleared for farms, roads, and homes, flowers often disappear. Wildflowers can be saved when land is set aside in parks and nature preserves. You can help in little ways by not picking wildflowers unless you are sure that they are abundant or weedy. Perhaps the best idea is to take nothing but photographs.

Deserts are dry places most of the year. Even the spring rain that falls in the Sonoran desert of Arizona and southeast California wets just the top few inches of soil. But cacti are well suited for life in dry surroundings. The saguaro is the giant cactus of the Sonoran desert. It grows to a height of 50 feet (15 meters), as tall as a telephone pole. The saguaro's roots spread far in all directions near the surface, often as far as the height of the plant. After a rain, the roots soak up water very quickly, carrying hundreds of gallons to the saguaro's stem. The saguaro grows very slowly, a few inches a year. The tallest plants may be 150 to 200 years old.

In the spring, the saguaro blossoms with long, tubular, showy flowers. Bats and moths and other insects visit the flowers at night to feed on the nectar and carry pollen from one plant to another. Woodpeckers dig out nests in the trunklike stems. Other birds, such as the curved-bill thrasher (shown here), spend much of their time on the saguaro.

The saguaro was, and still is, an important source of food and raw material for Native Americans who lived in the desert. They ate its red-pulped fruit raw and preserved it in a syrupy form for later eating. They made the juice into a drink and ground the seeds into a kind of butter. They made lodgepoles for their dwellings from the giant ribs of the saguaro and used the dried remains of dead plants as fuel.

In May or June, at a lake or a pond, clouds of winged insects may suddenly appear seemingly out of nowhere. For three or four days, masses of them cover trees, streetlights, and even people out for an evening walk. The insects are called mayflies, dayflies, or ephemera ("lasting but a day"). The photo shows mayflies on trees near Lake Dadanelle in Arkansas, but they often appear in cities near the Great Lakes, such as Chicago and Cleveland.

The swarming of mayflies is a mating dance and should naturally take place over streams and ponds but sometimes accidentally happens over city streets. Mayflies live for several days, just long enough to mate and lay eggs. Clusters of as many as four thousand eggs are dropped in fresh water. The clusters sink and soon hatch into gilled young called naiads or nymphs. The young look nothing like the adults. They live an underwater life that lasts from a few weeks to one, two, or even three years, swimming or crawling about on the bottom, feeding on tiny animals and decaying plant stems and leaves.

The naiads molt many times and pass through a winged stage, at which time they are called subimagos. They rise to the water surface, enclosed in a bubble of air, and fly to a nearby branch of a tree. Here they molt again and an adult, called an imago, emerges. The mating dances take place soon after the winged adults appear and the cycle of life starts again in the spring.

Spring never really reaches the high peaks of the Rocky Mountains or the Sierra Nevada. Snowfields and glaciers are found year-round at these elevations, where temperatures rarely rise above freezing even in summer. The upward limit of tree growth, called the timberline or tree line, is the point where cold temperatures, small amounts of rainfall, or poor soil prevent trees from growing.

Timberlines are usually lower on mountains in the North than in the South because temperatures are colder farther from the equator. Some mountains in the Rockies have two timberlines. Trees are scarce and small at the dry timberline because of little rainfall. A few thousand feet higher at the cold timberline, no trees grow at all.

In the West, moisture-laden winds from the Pacific Ocean blow against the western mountainsides. These windward slopes are usually more cloudy and rainy in the spring than the leeward slopes (facing east). On windward slopes near the tree line, trees known as elfinwood grow in strange and twisted shapes. Leeward slopes are drier and the tree line is higher because of the lack of rainfall. Along lower slopes of the western mountains, spring temperatures range from the warmth of New Mexico and Arizona to the still-chilly temperatures of Washington and Montana. In many places, mountain goats, bighorn sheep, and mountain lions move higher up when temperatures warm up.

Spring is the season to look for skunk cabbage shoots poking through the snow, to hear the early morning songs of robins and the late afternoon cackle of red-winged blackbirds, to feel the soft catkins of a pussy willow, to taste the first berries that ripen, and to smell the wet earth after a rain. Springtime is the sounds and sights of nature reawakening across America after the white sleep of winter snows.